Soul Scribbles

Soul Scribbles

Prakhar Verma

Published by Tablo

About the author

I'm a sentient being like you.

In the game of life, I'm a writer, coach, entrepreneur, lifelong learner, polymath, truth-seeker, and lover of life. I keep finding and creating myself over and over again, so I won't give myself any more titles.

My soul led me to create DesignEpicLife.com where I write articles and offer coaching services. After writing hundreds of articles and helping hundreds of people, my soul led me to publish this book.

Through this book, I fulfill my longing to connect with your soul. I dedicate this book to you.

– Prakhar Verma

Introduction

This book is a voice to my soul. It's not a how-to book, nor does it try to persuade you to believe anything. It's a collection of scribbles that my soul wanted to sing out loud.

As you read the scribbles, you may find peace in your mind and love in your heart. You may also dislike some or disagree with some. Whatever happens, take notice and reflect on how that scribble affects your soul.

You'll find that sometimes I'm writing to your soul directly even if we haven't met. If you look for the message, you'll find it. Don't wait for too long if you feel inspired to apply a message to your life.

You can read the scribbles one after another or one a day in any order you like. You can read the book regardless of your spiritual or religious beliefs. All you need is an open mind and an open heart.

The slower you read, the more you'll immerse yourself in the book and absorb the messages. Come back to this book and open a random page whenever you feel like doing so.

Forget your personality

The moment you give yourself a title, an identity, or a personality, you trap yourself into an outlook.

Your individuality is so unique that it can't be captured into a preexisting title. No one like you has come before, and no one will ever be like you.

Escape all categories that society wants you to fit into. Titles are for the unfree. Be free. Be who you are.

They will hate you for your love

The more loving you become, the more hatred you'll get. People can't stand love because they don't think they're worthy of love.

Love is for everyone. You don't need to become worthy of it. Your existence itself is an act of love. Before you can let others love you, you need unconditional love from yourself.

Once you've loved yourself unconditionally, you can extend that love to everyone. Then again, people will hate you for loving them. But that shouldn't affect your love for them.

Your unconditional love is for everyone. Self-love and love toward others are the same. Loving yourself means loving the entire world.

The measure of your life

You can measure your life by the number and the depth of transformations you go through.

You can't transform until you take the leap of faith. You can't transform until you face the demons. You can't transform until you feel the pain.

The sea of transformation is calling you to adventure. Why are you still sitting? What are you waiting for?

You've already lost what you have to lose. You have everything to gain out there.

You'll find what you look for

Look at the stars. They'll align for you if you look for a beautiful pattern. But if you look for chaos, all you'll find is a gigantic mess.

Look at the strangers. They'll show their best traits if you look for them. But if you only look for their poor traits, all you'll find is a wasted person.

Look at your life. It will be full of riches if you look for gratitude. But if you only focus on what you lack, all you'll feel is a deep sense of dissatisfaction.

"Love-play" is all there is

Everything can be distilled down to love and play.

It's all a game of love we're playing together. Some are ahead; some are lost behind.

But there is no competition because everyone is playing their part. It's exactly how it's meant to be.

The great puzzle of life

Life constantly throws puzzles at you. When you find an answer to one question, ten more questions emerge.

The quality of your life depends on the questions you ask yourself. The beauty of life does not necessarily lie in finding answers. It comes from asking the right questions.

The act of looking for answers is enough to live a fulfilling life. Your job is not to find a solution. It is to live the puzzle of life.

Being at peace

Everyone wants peace. Yet we're deprived of it because it slips through our fingers whenever we try to grasp it. The moment you get it, you lose it to another drama in your life.

The price of peace is chaos. If you want true peace, no amount of "chilling" will bring it to you. Peace comes from within when you train yourself in the playground of life.

Inner work, combined with chaos, is how you get better at being at peace. Instead of getting an instant moment of relief, delay the gratification and face your shadows to attain true peace.

Free to think

The easiest way to trap your thinking is to believe in something.

If you consciously believe in something to help yourself, that's another matter. But if you believe in something as if you know the truth, then you'll never be free to think.

When you're free of beliefs, you become free to think.

Freethinkers aren't interested in beliefs or facts. They enjoy learning about religion as much as they enjoy science. They enjoy the art of thinking and use it as a tool for creativity.

They aren't afraid to contradict themselves. They can change their minds. They don't take thoughts or beliefs seriously. They're free to express themselves. They're free to think.

Who am I?

Your identity is an illusion. It's made up of titles given by society.

The question itself is a waste. A better question is—who am I not?—the answer to which has no end.

The more you know who you're not, the more you'll find who you are.

Your anxiety is comedy

The sooner you realize that all your anxieties are actually comedies, the sooner you'll be liberated from them.

You think your anxieties are unique, but I hate to break this to you—we all are going through the same shit because we have the same primal fears.

I'm not saying that you don't have it bad. All I'm saying is that people have had it worse, and life still goes on.

Your anxiety is a comedy, and so is mine. Let's laugh together!

These two words are enough

Say, "Thank you," to anything and everything that happens — the good and the bad.

Say, "Thank you," to everyone who exists — the moral person and the immoral person.

Say, "Thank you," to yourself — your shadows and your gifts.

Everything is perfect just as it is. Your judgment is not needed. All that is needed are two words — thank you.

Leave room for possibilities

Protect your time, money, energy, and attention. But leave some room for possibilities where you can risk your resources to explore.

Exploration can help you discover new realities and reach new dimensions. Know when to stay in your bubble and when to break out of it. Every possibility comes with its risk and reward.

Explore, set up camp, and then explore again.

What are you afraid of, really?

No, really — what are you afraid of?

What you're afraid of is absurd. Just think for a second — if your fears came true, then what? Yeah, you will suffer the consequences, but then what?

I'm not saying that you should do everything you're afraid of. What I'm saying is quite the opposite. Do what you love so much that fear doesn't matter anymore.

Stop selling yourself short because of fear. Sell yourself to the universe. Show us what you've got. Be fearless.

Effortless productivity

You work hard because you're supposed to work hard. And because hard work feels hard, you hate it. Then you feel guilty about procrastinating, slacking off, and being lazy.

In reality, procrastination is natural. It is happening all the time because when you're choosing to do something, you're also choosing not to do something else.

High performance also comes naturally when you're aligned with your life force and intuition. When you combine that power with the core principles of productivity, you become an unstoppable force of nature.

The lost source of love

Selfishness and selflessness are one thing when their purpose is to create love. It's like a relationship between two individuals who complement each other fully.

Your capacity to love depends on the relationship between selfishness and selflessness within you. The deeper the bond, the more you can love.

Instead of picking between selfishness and selflessness, try bonding the lost soulmates. You'll never run out of love to give.

The whole point of life

Treat the entire universe—your life, all facts, all science, all people, all self-help books—as fiction.

Fiction leaves space for imagination, discovery, creativity, invention, innovation, exploration, mystery, magic, awe, and wonder.

When you limit yourself with pure logic or any belief system, you shut down the whole point of life, which is to experience it.

Life is evolving, and yet you cling to what is.

The best religion

Instead of following every piece of advice from all the successful people, listen to your own inner wisdom and learn from your own life experiences.

There's only one religion worth following, i.e. the religion of self. Do what helps you without harming others. Experiment with yourself to come to your own conclusions.

Use other's experiences as stories to learn from, but always come back to your own truth. No one else can give you the cheat codes to your life.

The flow of love

We're not very good at letting love flow from one person to another. In fact, we don't even let love flow among ourselves.

The key to the endless flow of love is when you love yourself and others, even when they don't show the same love to you or to themselves.

Unconditional self-love becomes the eternal passage through which everything that passes becomes love.

The importance of death

If you want to breathe in, you must breathe out.

If you want to eat, you must empty your stomach.

If you want to get something, you must let go of something else.

If you want to live, you must die.

To deny death is to deny life.

Unlimited willpower

Under normal circumstances, you don't need the willpower to breathe, eat, or sleep. Everything happens naturally when you let it.

When you do things that are aligned with your path, everything happens naturally. Effort becomes effortless. Time becomes timeless. You dissolve into nothingness.

To live an extraordinary life, live normally. Abnormal living happens in accordance with society. Normal living happens in accordance with your soul.

The purpose of your eyes

Look at the sun.

It gives, knowing that you can't give it anything in return. It illuminates everything it touches. It's a pure form of unconditional love.

The job of your eyes is the same as the sun — to love everything and everyone they see as it is; to illuminate love so that all judgments disappear as darkness disappears in the presence of light.

Through your eyes, you can change the world.

The death of everything

The death of a leaf is not the end of the tree; a new leaf is born.

The death of a tree is not the end of the forest; a new tree is born.

The death of a forest is not the end of the animals; a new forest is born.

The death of an animal is not the end of the ecosystem; a new animal is born.

The death of an ecosystem is not the end of life; a new ecosystem is born.

The death of life is not the end of the earth; a new life is born.

The death of the earth is not the end of the universe; a new planet is born.

The death of the universe is not the end of eternity; a new universe is born.

The forest of life

There are three kinds of people in the forest of life.

Lost
They are lost. They don't know what to do or where to go.
They're breathing, but they aren't living.

Follower
They follow the guidance of people who claim to know how to
navigate the forest. The trouble is that they follow a path walked
by someone else in order to get something. They lose the
purpose of the forest, which is to create their own path and fully
experience it.

Explorer
They are truly living. Their future is uncertain. They're not lost
because they know what they're looking for. To explore new
possibilities, they are willing to face their fears and take risks.
They'll probably take more time to reach their destination than a
follower, but they're willing to make that sacrifice because their
reward is not waiting at the destination. Their reward is in
carving their own path.

Who would you choose to be?

The possibility zone

Get out of your bubble of certainty. You've stayed there enough.
It has served you well, but it's time you go out.

I know you love your bubble because it seems riskier to go out
and explore. But by not taking that risk, you're already tying
chains to yourself. The longer you stay, the more chains will
tangle you up.

The vastness of life awaits you. New places, new people, new
experiences, new stories, and new lessons are calling you to
explore.

All you have to do is leave your bubble.

The depth of your life

Everyone wants to live longer. But rarely does anyone talk about living a deeper life. You don't need a long life to experience your aliveness.

You don't need to read research papers to know how to increase the depth of your life. Go deep inside yourself.

The more you get in touch with your inner self, the deeper you'll live. Magical experiences will emerge from your perception of reality. Life will reward you immensely with its richness.

You can't fully control the length of your life, but you can fully control its depth.

Let life shock you

You avoid emotional and spiritual shocks to avoid pain. When it arrives, you do everything to deny it. You want to feel good, so you find a distraction.

But how long will you keep running away? Eventually, the shock will strike you. The longer you hide, the stronger it gets.

Stop resisting the shock. Yes, it will hurt, but it's for your own good. The shock is the medicine for your wounds.

Give yourself permission to feel terrible after getting hit by a shock. That's when you know you've taken the first step toward healing.

The courage to love

Love takes courage because its direct opponent is fear. All love starts with self-love, so it distills down to the courage to love yourself.

Guilt and shame will act as hands of fear, stopping you from loving yourself. You will feel dirty and selfish for loving yourself. But if you keep loving yourself, you will come to the place of pure self-love. A love of this kind multiplies when it touches others.

Have the courage to love yourself because self-love is the source of all love. Loving others without loving yourself is like a beggar trying to donate money. Become rich and abundant with self-love, so you can give it as much as you want.

A useless mind

An occupied mind may fuel productivity but it lowers creativity. An empty mind prepares you for productivity and enhances creativity. Without periods of empty mind, an occupied mind is useless.

Your so-called relaxation is a distraction in disguise. Real relaxation comes from non-doing and non-thinking states. How often do you empty your mind so it can be filled again?

New thoughts require emptiness. Breakthroughs come to those who create the space to receive them.

Let your mind be silent.

Unspoken laws of nature

A horse doesn't celebrate the song of a bird. A bat doesn't wake up to the alarm of the hen.

A painter doesn't hear what a musician can listen to. A dancer doesn't think what a writer can imagine.

A child doesn't know about the responsibilities of life. An adult doesn't remember what it was like to play.

The heart doesn't understand the chatter of the mind. The mind doesn't grasp the feelings of the heart.

Getting things done without doing

When you try to do so much, you end up doing nothing, or you do a mediocre job at best.

Instead of doing, if you focus on being in the moment, everything happens effortlessly. Showing up to the present task at hand, here and now, is the essence of being.

In that presence, doing happens through you. You melt into the present. The job gets done as you lose the sense of time. When it's done, you move on to the next thing the present moment brings.

The magic of awareness

Through awareness, every moment becomes productive; every experience becomes rich; every person becomes a part of you.

Silence becomes music. Noise becomes quiet.

The reality appears. The illusion disappears.

The self becomes the universe. You become selfless.

Love multiplies. Fear subsides.

Play and rest

You're here to play and rest, not to work and burn out. A playful and restful life is the way to peace and happiness.

Society will convince you that work and burnout are the realities of life. But you can be free of that conditioning only if you refuse to walk down that path.

Health, wealth, relations, happiness, growth — they all are life's games. Abundance comes to you when you play for fun.

Sometimes, you win. Sometimes, you lose. In between the games, you take all the rest you need.

The pleasure of pain

Pain, struggle, suffering, and discomfort hurt. A lot.

Heartbreak, loss, rejection, and abandonment hurt. A lot.

Change, tragedy, defeat, and emptiness hurt. A lot.

As a protective mechanism, you want to avoid them to maximize pleasure. But the more you fight or hide, the more painful it gets. Over time, your safety net gives rise to depression and anxiety.

There's only one way out of the loop, which is the way of surrender. When you surrender, the pain doesn't go away, but pain and pleasure become two sides of the same coin. That's when you experience the beauty of life and the richness of being alive.

Set your soul free

We're little creatures made of love and fear.

By default, you're programmed to choose fear. The more you live in the default state, the more your consciousness diminishes.

Therefore, you dig an even deeper hole for yourself. The hole keeps you secure. And because security feels good, you keep yourself in it. But if you gather the courage to choose love, your consciousness evolves.

Slowly, you come out of the hole to experience the world of liberty. You can stay in the hole of security, or you can evolve to experience liberty. The hole of security keeps your ego protected, but it kills your soul.

Liberty demands short-term pain and extreme courage, but it sets your soul free for eternity.

Becoming wise

The best way to gain knowledge is to teach it. The best way to gain skill is to practice it. The best way to gain wisdom is to experience it.

Teachers can help you with knowledge and skills, but they can't help you with wisdom. They can drop hints and tell stories about their journey, but you must find your own wisdom.

Wisdom is unique to every person. You can only learn it through your own experience. Once learned, you can't transfer it to another person.

True wisdom begins when you drop all the books, gurus, teachers, and mentors. Mindful experience is the highest form of wisdom.

Give to get

If you want to be healthy, give yourself the nourishment you need.

If you want to be wealthy, give your gift to the people who need it.

If you want to be happy, give happiness to others.

If you want to be loved, give your love to others.

If you want to live, give your gratitude to life.

Becoming you

From the moment you are born, you start becoming someone.
Every day, you lose yourself even more.

Your journey to true self starts the moment you turn back and
return to the path you came from. That's your home. That's who
you truly are.

When you come back to yourself, you become free. All the
masks and labels disappear.

Remember who you're not, and you will reach your destination.

Doing nothing

Having the time to do nothing is the new luxury of a rich life.

Doing nothing is like dating your soul. When you keep yourself busy all the time, you never take time for your soul. You know what happens when you stop dating your partner — they break up with you.

Don't ignore your soul. Your soul loves you. Love your soul back. Give it the time it deserves. Do nothing.

Life is not enough

Your lifetime is not enough to find all the answers you seek. But it's enough to ask as many questions as you want. Questions provoke curiosity, wonder, creativity, discovery, and meaning. That much is enough.

Your lifetime is not enough to achieve everything you desire. But it's enough to pursue what truly matters to you. Pursuit brings adventure, growth, focus, success, and fulfillment. That much is enough.

Your lifetime is not enough to experience everything you want. But it's enough to be present in your experiences. Presence produces love, peace, joy, abundance, and freedom. That much is enough.

Who are you?

Who are you without your job title?

Who are you without your wealth?

Who are you without your looks?

Who are you without your relationships?

Who are you without your skills?

Get naked. Take off your masks.

Forgetting who you are is the first step toward remembering who you truly are.

The secret to eternal life

You have a gift inside you, but that gift is wrapped up in a box.
Gifts are meant to be opened. It's your duty to unwrap it. At
first, you may open up the wrong boxes, but you must keep
going until you find your gift. When you've found it, you will
know it.

When you're in tune with your natural genius, your creative
potential explodes. Creativity merges with your existence. You
realize the function of your ego, which is to express and create.

You can only create until you die, but your gifts remain with the
universe forever. That's how you increase the depth of your
existence in the universe. Creativity allows you to make your
gifts eternal, even after your form disappears.

The best kind of personal growth

Personal growth is shallow without spiritual growth. Spiritual growth is empty without personal growth.

Personal growth and spiritual growth differ from each other, but they make a perfect pair.

Your ego needs personal growth. Your soul needs spiritual growth. If one grows without the other, the relationship breaks apart. They don't understand each other. They hate each other.

If they grow together, the relationship flourishes. They sing and dance together. They create magic together.

Your legend

We all have a legend. Your legend is different from mine, but we can be part of each other's legends.

A beautiful world is created through a harmonious bond of several legends. A world where we all thrive in our separate ways. A world where we all become successful in our own eyes. A world where we all allow each other to be who we are.

Let's create this new world. All you have to do is be your true self and do your real job, which are the simplest yet hardest tasks of all.

I wish you to live your legend. I promise I will live mine. Maybe one day, we'll cross paths.

This is your home

You have arrived at the present moment. There's nowhere else to go. This is your home.

There's nothing to seek, nothing to dwell on. There's nothing to anticipate, nothing to remember. This is your home.

The moment is filled with emptiness. The emptiness is filled with vastness. This is your home.

The ego is losing its senses. The present is becoming more real. O human, you have arrived. This is your home.

Do not follow my advice

My wisdom may not be your wisdom. Your wisdom may not be my wisdom. The best wisdom comes from self-knowledge and individual life experience.

Do not follow my advice. Follow your own advice along with me. After listening to me, do your own experiments and dig your own lessons.

I'm not the wisest person for you. I'm the wisest person for myself. You're the wisest person for you. If I provoke thinking in you, my job is done.

Now your job begins.

A simple way to succeed

When you're focusing, you're also distracting yourself. You can't focus on everything at once. If you distract yourself wisely, you focus better.

When you're being productive, you're also procrastinating. You can't do it all. If you procrastinate wisely, you get more done.

When you're succeeding, you're also sacrificing. You can't have it all at the same time. If you sacrifice wisely, you achieve more.

No goal

Plants have no goals. They keep on growing.

Animals have no goals. They keep on playing.

All goals of yours come from the expectations of others. You want to beat others, impress others, get their respect, or leave a legacy.

What goals would you have left if there was nobody to impress? You will come to your natural state of growth and play.

You can come back to your natural state even in the turmoil of this competitive culture. Don't let goals distract you from living your life in its pure form.

Lifelong learners don't die

Lifelong learning goes beyond reading books, taking courses, or listening to lectures. It is a way of being.

You are an open book where anything or anyone can write, but you decide what you want to keep in the final edited version.

If you're a lifelong learner, you're learning 24/7 — from your thoughts, from your emotions, from your meditations, from your dreams, from your daydreams, from your mentors, from your students, from your friends, from your enemies, from your experiences, from your work, from your mistakes, from your failures, from your rejections, from your successes, and from your higher self.

A lifelong learner can never die. They transcend to another person's open book to live the mysteries of life.

Give more than you get

There's an everyday battle you're fighting to get more. If you switch that battle to give more than you get, you'll get more than you can imagine.

If more people gave more than they get, the world would be an abundant place where everybody gives more, yet they all get more in return.

By getting this life, you've already won the lottery. Show your appreciation for life by giving as much as you can. You lack nothing, and you have everything to give.

Forget taking. Give and then receive to give even more.

Become inbound

Being outbound is when you're out there chasing what you want. Being inbound is when you let the thing come to you.

You'll get everything you want when you're ready to handle it. So instead of focusing on the thing you want, focus on getting stronger so you can hold it and on becoming the person who can keep it.

When you're the right person to get it, the thing itself will come running to you.

Life is a melody

Life is made of ups and downs. Sometimes, you're at the peak of ecstasy, while sometimes, you're in the depths of pain.

The beauty of the song is in the ears of the listener. If you can hear the music, every part of the song is in harmony.

Let loose and surrender to the song. Enjoy the tune because you can't listen to it again. This is your only chance.

You're the composer, you're the musician, and you're the listener. Escape into the song, and create a masterpiece.

Your illusory life

"Good and bad" or "negative and positive" don't exist in the universe's vocabulary. The universe only knows the language of unconditional, infinite love.

All your hopes, desires, fears, and frustrations are illusions. Let them be your entertainment, but don't get attached to them.

Think of them as a video game that you can turn off and come back to any time. Or think of them as a sport you watch for your enjoyment. Yeah, you will feel disappointed if you or your team loses, but it won't be the end of the world.

All the polarities exist in your mind. Don't take your thoughts too seriously. Don't take your emotions too seriously. Don't take your games too seriously. Don't take yourself too seriously. Don't take your life too seriously.

Your existence will end, but your love will last forever.

Fear vs. freedom

Freedom and courage go hand in hand. Through courage, you free yourself from the chains of fear.

You don't need confidence, logic, or motivation. Just lean toward the fear. You'll find that the thing you're afraid of is actually afraid of you. It's afraid of your potential when you become free.

Truly free people are hard to find. They are superhumans to the public. In reality, there's nothing super about them. They just recognized the illusion of fear and overcame it by facing it. They didn't wait for the stars to align. They live freely. They actualize their potential.

An easygoing life

You have all the choices in the world. So much so that you're now paralyzed.

You have all the information at your fingertips. So much so that you're now confused.

You have so much work to do. So much so that you're never done.

Today, the secret to living is elimination. Bring constraints and eliminate choices. The more choices you have, the more scattered your life becomes. The fewer choices you have, the easier your life flows.

Your natural state

Your natural state is of flow and creativity. When you're disconnected from it, you're distracted and wasted.

Your natural state is of giving and serving. When you're disconnected from it, you're taking and hoarding.

Your natural state is of joy and play. When you're disconnected from it, you're anxious and depressed.

Your natural state is of love and abundance. When you're disconnected from it, you hate and fear.

Close your eyes and come back to your natural state. Let the chaos and reactions settle to the bottom like mud in water. Your mind will become clear like water. Through this clear and empty mind, your natural state will arise.

Coherent living

Coherence is when your heart, soul, mind, and body work in harmony. The heart surrenders to the soul, the soul guides the mind, the mind signals the body, and the body does its job.

Such a beautiful union makes a man go beyond himself. He actualizes himself and transcends his ego. He enters into another dimension where the impossible becomes possible.

To enter a coherent state, you don't need to know anything. It's the opposite of knowing or believing. It's pure trust and surrender.

Your sexuality

Your sexuality is the source of energy. This life energy is the primary driver of all species.

If you're out of touch with your sexuality, you're disconnected from yourself. You'll have no drive. Without drive, there is no life.

Stop suppressing or abusing your sexuality. Both masculinity and femininity are within you. If you're male, attend to your masculine side and connect with your feminine side. if you're female, attend to your feminine side and connect with your masculine side.

The union of masculine and feminine is divine, whether it's between two individuals or happens within you.

Authentic living

Authentic living is the hardest and the simplest way to live. It's only hard until you've reached your authentic self. Once you're there, the path ahead looks utterly simple.

The path doesn't look like a track where people race against each other. Rather, it looks like an endless journey into the unknown.

When you walk on this path, you come out of your cocoon like a butterfly. You shed your old skin like a snake. You sing like a nightingale. You fly like a vulture. You roar like a lion. You die like a human who has truly lived.

Being human

Only a silent mind knows inner peace. Only a rebellious soul knows true freedom. Only a healthy body knows a virtuous character.

You can't blossom with a noisy mind, a trapped soul, or an unhealthy body. It is vital to take care of them because they are the foundations for being human. Only a blossoming person grows and contributes.

Press mute. Free yourself. Do your job.

The power of your thoughts

Every thought has four elements: polarity, intensity, focus, and repetition. The combination determines the impact of your thoughts.

The polarity of thought is the emotional charge on it. Positive thoughts create coherence and higher vibrations.

The intensity of thought is the amount of energy it carries. The greater the energy, the more significant and memorable it becomes.

The focus of thought is its subject. Thinking of ideas or imagining possibilities is better than self-centered or judgmental thinking.

The repetition of thought is the number of times you choose to think of the desired thought. Autosuggestion allows you to change your default thought pattern in the direction of your choice.

Your thought can be a weapon of destruction or a tool for evolution. You make the choice.

Helping yourself

Self-help is not found in books.

The only way to help yourself is to just do it. If you keep on
reading self-help books without helping yourself, you'll
accumulate worthless knowledge that may be impressive to talk
about, but it's of no real value.

The reason helping yourself is hard is that it's so simple. You
convince yourself that the answer to your problems must be
more complicated and harder to implement. So you keep seeking
more self-help books to solve the same problem. You get lost in
the maze of self-deception.

Books can give you clues, but they can't get you out of the maze
to the training ground of life. You must put that book down
to help yourself.

Your reality

A scientific fact may not be right. If it gets proven wrong tomorrow, it was never right.

A belief may not be right. If it gets proven wrong tomorrow, it wasn't right either.

Don't rely on facts or beliefs. They will keep changing as we keep exploring.

We may play in the same field with the same universal laws, but my reality is not your reality.

Don't let your intellect imprison you. It's full of unconscious biases that can give you faulty conclusions. Know that you don't know the reality. You can only experience your reality.

You have one job

Whatever pulls you away from the center of your being is a distraction. All the work, commitments, relationships, hobbies, habits, and activities you engage in exist to lead you toward one goal.

You may not understand where this drive comes from, but it's there for a reason. It wants you to come back to yourself. That's the ultimate goal.

It's easy to numb yourself if you don't know the goal. Even if you know the goal, it's easy to lose your way if you don't remember it.

You have only one full-time job. All the other jobs are temporary. Do your job well, and come back to yourself over and over again.

Let people hate you

Never betray your soul to please others. It doesn't matter if they are your parents, spouse, siblings, children, or friends. Be loyal to your soul.

If you don't stay true to your soul, you'll hate yourself and resent everyone. You'll live out of anger, hatred, sadness, and depression.

Love starts with the self. Respect and honor your soul to know how to love. You can only spread your love to others when you've learned the art of loving yourself.

Sometimes, the price of love is accumulating hatred from others. Let it be that way. Be a true lover.

Connecting with your soul

When you speak from your soul, your words create poems, and your silence creates songs. You sound wise to some and foolish to others.

When you look through your soul, all you see is truth and beauty. Your perception is accurate for some and invalid for others.

When you act in accordance with your soul, you do the right thing and give your best. Your actions seem heroic to some and evil to others.

When you listen to your soul, the world opens all doors to you and gives you everything you desire. You look prosperous to some and greedy to others.

All you need is a moment of silence

A moment of silence is all you need.

A moment of silence is an empty yet also a fulfilling act.

A moment of silence is an easy yet also a difficult act.

A moment of silence is a simple yet also a skillful act.

A moment of silence is a selfish but also a selfless act.

A moment of silence is a distant yet also a loving act.

A moment of silence is a mindful yet also a mindless act.

A moment of silence is all you need.

Free yourself

People are trying to put you into a box. To be accepted, you stay locked in your box. If you dare to come out, people will hate you and try to drag you down.

The past is trying to put chains on you. To be safe, you remain chained to your prison. If you dare to break free, the past will follow you and try to haunt you.

The mind is trying to program you. To be entertained, you accept the illusions as truths. If you dare to switch off the television, the mind will switch to another channel and try to distract you.

You can be where you are. Or you can be free. Escape from the box, break up the chains, and switch off the television.

It's still not too late

There's still time for you to explore your potential.
There's still time for you to be yourself.
There's still time for you to create.
There's still time for you to grow.
There's still time for you to love.
There's still time for you to live.
There's still time for you to be free.
There's still time for you to transcend.
There's still time for you to raise your consciousness.

There's still plenty of time, but not enough time if you don't take the first step now. If you take the first step, the universe will take ten steps for you.

lationship between your heart and mind

't is a fool to the mind. The mind is a fool to the heart.
ver seem to stop fighting with each other.

1 both the mind and the heart open up, they understand
er. That's the only way to make the relationship work.

ur mind. Open your heart. Become whole.

Your choice

You can be safe, or you can live.
You can resist, or you can accept.
You can suffer, or you can surrender.
You can be attached, or you can be free.
You can fit in, or you can be yourself.
You can despair, or you can trust.
You can judge, or you can love.

You choose.

Your real purpose

Love is energy. It flows from one person to another. All problems arise when the flow of energy is blocked.

The blockage may be small, but it has tremendous implications because it breaks the chain of love. It prevents the energy to pass along the endless chain.

When you find the blockage in you, clear it up. Start new chains of love through your thoughts, emotions, words, and actions.

Your job may be different from mine. But we're all here to do the same work. Take small actions toward the big cause of love. That is our real purpose.

You versus fear

It's natural to have fears. But don't be
safe in the hands of fear. The real terr
your fears.

If you get scared, fear becomes strong
its power. The fear doesn't go away, b
The fear no longer controls you.

When you become full of love, fear b
you lean into it, it has no choice but t
your fears work together as a team. L
You ride the fear, and the fear guides

The

The h
They

But w
each o

Open

The dichotomies of life

Peace is found in chaos.

Bliss is found in suffering.

Gratitude is found in loss.

Love is found in hate.

Freedom is found in bondage.

Finding the truth

What if we listen, ask, and express instead of defending, attacking, and manipulating in our conversations?

There is more to a conversation than being right or wrong. We all can be a little more right, one conversation at a time if we open our minds and hearts because that's when we get the chance to see other realities.

The combination of distinct realities helps us identify the limits in our perception. Then we can see the truth.

The awakening trap

When you experience awakenings, it's easy to abandon the game of life.

The point of awakenings is not to withdraw from the game, but it is to train yourself to realize that you are beyond the game. You can pause the game any time you want by distancing yourself as you remember the truth.

Games are for experiences and expressions. Have fun playing the games, but then come back. Don't let the awakenings or the games pull you to one side. Do a little dance with life.

A clouded mind

When the clouds appear, you don't try to control them. You wait for them to pass, knowing that the sun is behind them.

When your canvas is heavily clouded with thoughts, emotions, and sensations, there's no need to control them. You know that the sun is still present.

Enjoy the view as it is. Rejoice when the sky is clear and you can see the sun again.

The chain of love

The sun sends love to the earth.

Earth passes that love so that plants can be born.

Plants pass that love so that we can be born.

Our job is to pass that love on to one another.

Even when the sun goes down, love remains. Even when you die, your love will remain.

Come back home

Come back home after playing outside. Most people play for too long and never come back. They forget they were playing so they live in illusions.

When you remember to keep coming back, you develop a sense of home and play no matter where you are. You don't get lost because you cultivate your home wherever you go and play whenever you want.

Keep coming back until your home and the playground become one.

Take off your masks

If you keep wearing masks, you'll forget who you are. You don't need to hide behind masks.

Instead, acknowledge the roles you need to play by wearing hats. Hats are different because, when you wear a hat, you act a role in the play of life.

Then you take them off when you need to with no trouble. You can switch the hats easily and quickly. You don't confuse them with your identity.

Self-judgment

All judgment is self-judgment. You then judge yourself for
judging others, which is meta self-judgment.

The judgment dissolves and the separation resolves in the
presence of compassion and understanding.

You become love. You become one.

Be an adult

The mind goes around in circles. The heart beats fast. The body freezes or freaks out.

You can wait for them to come back to normal, or you can bring them back to coherence at your command.

The mind needs a toy. The heart needs some love. The body needs safety.

They're all children, but you are an adult.

Just take the next step

Take one step at a time at your own pace. Focus on your own steps.

Let go of the trail you've left behind. Don't worry about the path ahead. Be here now and take your next step.

There's no need to rush. You will go far, and you will enjoy every step along the way.

That's the secret to being present and living life fully.

Create new thoughts

Your thoughts originate from the questions you ask yourself. If you want to have better quality thoughts, ask yourself better questions.

Trust the creativity of your mind to seek the answers you're looking for. It isn't always about finding the answers, though.

Even when you don't get the answer, you'll get something much better than your habitual thoughts.

Creating new thoughts is the simplest yet the most magnificent form of creativity because it gives birth to imagination and curiosity.

What new question will you ask yourself?

The traps of life

The more real illusions look to you, the more you get lost in the game.

The more you take life seriously, the more miserable you become.

The more you get attached to the things you don't really possess, the more you suffer.

The more opinions you care about, the more you lose yourself.

The more you resist the present, the more you miss the experience of being alive.

Dance with the universe

Set intentions, and then let life unfold as it does.

Seek answers, and then let the answers come to you.

Go for what you want, and then wait to get what you need.

Visualize your dream life, and then appreciate the life you're living.

Listen to me

If you want to listen to me, don't judge as I talk to you. Don't agree, disagree, like, or dislike. If you really want to judge, you can do so later when the show is over. But first, listen.

Listening is a miraculous opportunity for you to explore a different reality without entering another body. It's a way of experiencing life through the eyes of another human.

Empty your mind, and enter a new dimension. There's a different world on the other side.

Create space

If you want something better in life, you need to provide space for it to come.

You can't keep living the same way and wait for things to change. You must destroy to create space for something new.

New experiences, thoughts, and transformations are waiting for you. All you've got to do is create space for them.

Lift the veil of separation

Imagine every person as a copy of you. See them as if they are
you, but they are wearing a different skin and living a different
life.

How would you treat them differently? How would you
understand them differently? How would you love them
differently?

That's exactly how it is, but we fail to see it behind the curtain of
forms and personalities. Look at what's behind the curtain.

Try to understand

The social game is about the art of understanding.

We all speak different languages. Each of us has a unique perception and expression.

The more you understand others, the more you understand yourself. The more you understand yourself, the more you understand others.

The more you understand the whole, the more you can be at ease.

Become attractive

Approval is a drug.

It sure feels good, but you're attached to it, and you'll keep seeking more of it. You'll never get enough of it.

You can seek approval, or you can be attractive. Once you find your dignity, your self-love becomes so apparent that other people can't help but be attracted to you.

They may like you or dislike you, but you don't need their approval, and that's what makes you attractive. Your unconditional love gives them permission to love themselves.

Wise living

Live your life slowly but urgently.

Live your life simply but richly.

Have patience, but keep moving.

Do not rush, but do not settle.

Do not take life seriously, but live it wholeheartedly.

The quest for truth

If you're serious about finding the truth, you must be willing to face your illusions. You must be willing to find the lies. You must be willing to be wrong. You must be willing to change. You must be willing to look stupid. You must be willing to start again.

Observe your ego

When you're playing with your ego, make sure it's not the one in charge.

The ego will find sneaky ways to trick you into believing that it's in your control. That way, it finds another way to be in charge.

Watch your ego. Don't take your eyes off it. That's the only way to be in charge.

Real love

Go beyond self-love, romantic love, or any kind of sentient love.

Real love is to be yourself. Being yourself is your supreme task. Having your needs met will allow you to be yourself. Everything else is a by-product.

Real love isn't about you. Being yourself is like being the sun. It's an energetic expression of your form in this world. Everything else is secondary.

Real love is permanent. It lasts for an eternity and expands into infinity. You may not exist, but the love you create lasts forever. Everything else is temporary.

Be a love warrior. Be yourself.

Be ready

Wake up!

Death is coming. You have so much love to give. Squeeze out the juice from the life you have left.

Become so full of love and life that when death comes to see you, you will be ready to go home.

Die to live

Don't wait for death to be born again.

You can drop your past, programming, worries, regrets, anxieties, future, goals, hopes, desires, fears, and ego at any instant to reset your life.

Let the time stop so you can live in this eternal present. When you live in the moment, you forget about yourself. Then you're free to play and ready to love.

Don't hoard thoughts

Break the thread of thoughts. Your life situation and stories are all in your mind.

Take a break.

Give your mind something else to hold on to. Let the present thought go. Step away. Change the inputs. Think of something new. Shock your life.

Repeat until your mind is empty.

100

What a moment!

Moments give you the opportunity to train your human form and to let your soul play.

When you do that fully, you realize that everything else that happens is not in your control, or it's the byproduct of playing and training.

Abandon your plans. Release your past. Jump into the present. What a moment to train! What a moment to play!

Be selfish

Giving is as selfish as getting. So be selfish. Being selfish isn't bad. What's not good is living without compassion.

Compassion doesn't include a balance sheet of giving and taking. Compassion is the natural state of human beings.

When you enjoy living, love arises. Selfishness and compassion are part of living naturally.

Live selfishly and love unconditionally, both together.

Total abundance

What makes you anxious could also make you excited. What disappoints could also make you happy. What worries you could also make you hopeful.

Your feelings are polarized by the same things. They are two sides of the same coin.

Keep tossing the coin until the coin disappears into the abundant sky where all polarities dissolve into totality.

Let the universe lead you

The universe takes your wishes as commands only if you follow its lead.

To follow the universe's lead, be relaxed in your body, silent in your mind, and listen with your heart. The universe will lead you to the next step, but it won't give you the full map.

Follow the lead with complete trust.

Open your heart

Inhale love; exhale love.

Love is infinite. The mind's idea of love can distract you from all the other forms of love you constantly receive.

You can only give love when you're full of it. Open your heart to all forms of love, and you will never be out of love. Love will overflow and radiate through you in all directions.

The end of a beginning

Thank you for taking the time for your soul. This is where the book ends, but our journey begins.

If you enjoyed the book, consider the following:

1. Get occasional *Soul Reminders* in your inbox by subscribing to the Soul Scribbles email newsletter. You'll also get notified when I release the second book in the series.
   Go to: https://designepiclife.com/soul-reminders
2. Leave an honest review on Amazon (or at the online store where you bought this book).
   Go to: https://designepiclife.com/soul-review
3. Share it with your friends by sending them to https://designepiclife.com/soul-scribbles

To get in touch with me personally, you can contact me on my website DesignEpicLife.com where you'll also find free articles and information about my coaching service.

Until next time, keep this book with you and come back to it whenever you like.